FESTIVE BREADS of CHRISTMAS

Norma Jost Voth

Illustrated by Ellen Jane Price

HERALD PRESS
Scottdale, Pennsylvania
Waterloo, Ontario

Library of Congress Cataloging in Publication Data

Voth, Norma Jost.
  Festive breads of Christmas.

  Includes index.
  1. Bread   2. Christmas cookery.   I. Title.
TX769.V66 1983   641.8'15   82-15731
ISBN 0-8361-3319-6 (pbk.)

The paper used in this publication is recycled and meets the
minimum requirements of American National Standard for
Information Sciences—Permanence of Paper for Printed
Library Materials, ANSI Z39.48-1984.

FESTIVE BREADS OF CHRISTMAS
Copyright © 1983 by Herald Press, Scottdale, Pa. 15683
  Published simultaneously in Canada by Herald Press,
  Waterloo, Ont. N2L 6H7. All rights reserved.
Library of Congress Catalog Card Number: 82-15731
International Standard Book Number: 0-8361-3319-6
Printed in the United States of America

99 98 97 96 95 94 93 13 12 11 10 9 8 7
21,000 copies in print

*To my dear daughter, Susan, with the hope
that you may one day carry on this old
tradition of baking Christmas bread.*

Special thanks to Adaline Karber, who caters wedding receptions in San Jose, California, and to Samuel Kirk, career counselor and bread baking instructor, Denver, Colorado, for testing and evaluating Christmas bread recipes.

Thanks to Ellen Jane Price, teacher, and friend, for illustrating and decorating the pages in this series of holiday books, and to my husband, Alden, for encouragement, as well as eating and critiquing Christmas baking seven days a week.

Gratitude to Catherine Weidner (Moravians); Kaethe Warkentin, Bertha Harder (Russian Mennonites); Marthe Nussbaumer (Alsace); Margaret Kulish (Austria); Terttu Gilbert (Finland); Doris Walter, Elisabeth Mödlhammer (Germany); Kristina Scamagus (Greece); Iren Romoda (Hungary); Matilde Oliverio (Italy); Liesel Widmer, Erika Nussbaumer, Lilly Gyger, the baking staff of the Bienenberg Bible School (Switzerland); Liz Nelson (Norway); Margit Carlson (Sweden); Sonja Los Shore (Ukraine).

Festive Breads of Christmas

Our great-grandmothers, like generations of busy women before them, baked literally tons of dark, wholesome bread. Families were large. There were no corner bakeries. So bread was routinely baked at home—through good times and bad.

However, on holidays, especially Christmas and Easter, bread became more than nourishment—it became part of the family celebration.

From the pantry women brought their finest white flour (considered a luxury), gathered the freshest eggs from the barn, dipped generously into their butter churns, carried from the attic choicest dried fruits and nuts stored from harvest. They took saffron and spice from the cupboard.

Not enough, these extravagant ingredients. Women added yet another message: The shape of the bread must tell something of the religious meaning of the day. German mothers formed *Stollen* and *Fatschenkinder* to resemble a swaddling child. Ukrainians braided a royal three-tiered *Kolach*, ancient symbol of the Trinity and eternity. To the finished loaves they added a sprinkling of sugar or nuts, sculptured delicate flowers, birds, or a cross made from the dough.

Our great-grandmothers baked festive breads not as a chore, but with great joy. Sometimes they carried their bread to church to be blessed. To all they proclaimed: My gift of bread belongs to this holy season. It, too, is set apart from the simple, ordinary fare of every day.

On Christmas Eve the women proudly placed their loaves in the center of the table on the finest embroidered cloth, reserved for such days.

For centuries these beautiful breads have been a part of the Christmas season, adding dignity and meaning to the days of celebration. May they bring pleasure in your home as they do in ours.

Norma Jost Voth
San Jose, California

The Moravian Lovefeast

Moravian families look forward to a special children's lovefeast in their churches on Christmas Eve. In the tradition of the early church, they celebrate a "feast of love"—worship, music, and a simple meal together several times a year. Baskets of buns and mugs of coffee are served to everyone during the congregational singing.

Catherine Weidner recalls a time "when even the very young children were allowed to drink the mug of coffee at the lovefeast. . . . For as devoted Moravian parents said, 'Lovefeast coffee never hurt anyone!' It was quite a treat to be so 'grown up' several times a year. Now the children are served a cookie and mugs of chocolate milk.

"One of the three candle vigils on Christmas Eve is designated as the children's lovefeast. Lighted candles, symbols of Christian love and light, are passed to everyone in the congregation."

Catherine Weidner, Bethlehem, Pennsylvania, shares an old family recipe (p. 8) for these traditional Moravian Lovefeast Buns.

Moravian Lovefeast Buns

Candlelight lovefeasts, commemorating the birth of Christ, have been a tradition of the Moravian Church for more than 200 years. The first American lovefeast and candle service was held in Pennsylvania in 1756. Lovefeast buns and coffee are served to the congregation on Christmas Eve.

1 cup hot, dry mashed
  potatoes, unseasoned
2 pkg. active dry yeast
½ cup lukewarm water
1 tsp. sugar
½ cup butter
1 cup sugar

½ cup lukewarm milk
2 eggs, beaten
¼ tsp. nutmeg
½-1 tsp. mace
2 tbsp. grated orange
  peel
2 tbsp. orange juice
5-5½ cups flour

Pare, slice, and boil 2 or 3 potatoes. Mash and cool to lukewarm. (You may also use 1 cup prepared dry, quick, mashed potatoes.) Dissolve yeast in warm water and sugar. Cream butter and sugar together. Add mashed potatoes and mix well. Add lukewarm milk, eggs, yeast, seasonings, orange juice, and peel; mix well. Gradually add 2½ cups sifted flour and beat 5 minutes with electric mixer. Gradually add 2¼-2½ cups flour.

Turn out onto floured board and knead until smooth and elastic, about 8-10 minutes. Place in greased bowl, turning to grease top of dough. Cover with plastic wrap and let rise in warm place until doubled in bulk (about 1½ hours). Punch down and let rise a second time (40-45 minutes). Punch down.

Pinch off balls of dough (3 oz.) about the size of golf balls. Form into bun shape and place on greased baking sheet about 1½ inches apart. Flatten slightly. Cover with kitchen towel and let rise in warm place until doubled in size. Brush tops with melted butter or 1 egg beaten with 1 tsp. water. Bake at 350° about 15 minutes or until golden brown. Cover with towel to cool and soften. Makes 1½ dozen large buns.

COME LORD JESUS
OUR GUEST TO BE
AND BLESS THESE
GIFTS BESTOWED
by THEE. Amen

Grandmother called these coffee buns Russian Peppernuts. Russian—because it was one of the recipes her family brought from the Molotschna Colony (Ukraine) in Russia when the Mennonites settled on the plains of Kansas in 1874.

Traditionally the buns were sweetened with the much-loved watermelon syrup, plentiful because watermelons grew profusely in the rich Ukrainian soil. Hence they are also called Syrup Peppernuts, especially among the Mennonites in Canada. (Dark corn syrup and molasses have since replaced watermelon syrup.)

"My grandmother's peppernuts were raised with yeast, were high, light, and placed close together on the pan," says Miriam Penner Schmidt. From the yeast leavening they take another name—*Häv Päpanät*, Low German for Yeast Peppernuts.

The peppernut Christmas cookie tradition probably came with the Mennonites when they migrated from Holland to West Prussia to the Ukraine. Peppernut buns use some of the traditional cookie spices (often cinnamon and black pepper°) but are raised with yeast.

After the famine (1920s) in Russia, sugar, butter, cream—all the good baking ingredients—were scarce. Women baked their delicacies with whatever was available. "Mother flavored hers with fennel from the garden. If she was feeling particularly luxurious, she might brush the tops with a little egg," remembers Kaethe Kasdorf Warkentin.

These simple, tasty coffee buns, a unique ethnic product of Russian Mennonite kitchens, are baked not only at Christmas but year-round as well.

° Earlier pepper was the most expensive and highly prized of spices. The term pepper was used to mean not only black peppercorns but other spices as well.

Suse Toews' Russian Peppernuts

A Christmas specialty of Russian Mennonite kitchens, these high, light, spicy coffee buns bring back a host of nostalgic memories. The recipe comes from Suse Toews, Asuncion, Paraguay.

1 cup milk
½ cup margarine
½ cup brown sugar
½ tsp. salt
1½ pkg. active dry yeast
½ cup lukewarm water
2 tsp. sugar
½ cup dark Karo syrup
   or molasses
½ tsp. cinnamon
½ tsp. white pepper
¾ tsp. ground star anise°
4½-5 cups flour
Powdered Sugar Frosting

Over medium heat, blend milk, margarine, sugar, salt. Add syrup or molasses. Cool to lukewarm. Dissolve yeast in warm water and sugar. Combine milk and yeast mixtures. Add spices. Gradually add 2½ cups sifted flour and beat 5 minutes with electric mixer. Gradually add 2-2½ cups flour. Turn out onto floured board and knead until smooth and elastic, about 8-10

°You may substitute 1 tsp. crushed anise seed or 1 tsp. anise extract.

minutes. Place in greased bowl, turning to grease top of dough. Cover with plastic wrap and set in warm place to rise until doubled in bulk. Punch down. Pinch off balls of dough the size of large golf balls. Shape into buns and place close together on greased baking pans. Cover and let rise in warm place until doubled in size. Brush with melted margarine. Bake at 375° for 25-30 minutes or until golden brown. Cool on rack and cover with towel to soften. Makes 2½ dozen large buns.

Powdered Sugar Frosting: Combine 1 cup sifted confectioners' sugar, 1½ tbsp. milk, and ½-1 tsp. maple or vanilla flavoring.

o   o   o

Suse Toews is one of the many heroic women who suffered through World War II. After losing her father, husband, and brother in Russia, Mrs. Toews shepherded her aged mother, her brother's crippled wife, and five little children on foot from Russia to Germany, where she lived and cooked for refugees in a camp. Later in her new home in Paraguay, she continued cooking at the Mennonite Central Committee headquarters in Asuncion, all the while caring for her mother and raising her nieces and nephews. Now in her 70s, Mrs. Toews still cooks, bakes, and regularly sings in the church choir. A sample of her baking is the recipe above.

How Beautiful It Was!

"I remember one year we went to the church Christmas program by sleigh. Dad filled it with straw and we children crawled under buffalo robes and wool comforters," reflects (Aunt) Minnie Jost Krause, Hillsboro, Kansas. "Mother sat up front beside Dad, with the baby in her arms. I lay there, looking up at the stars, thinking about the program, and listening to the sleigh bells in the quiet night. How beautiful it was!

"At church each of us received gift sacks filled with candy, nuts, cookies, an orange, and apple. On the way home we were counting and smelling our treats when the horses hit a big drift, floundered, and the sleigh tipped over. All we children worried about was our candy. Nothing else mattered! ... On New Year's Day they dismantled the big tree at church, and of course, we couldn't miss that, so we walked to town along the railroad tracks to be there. We usually came home with an orange, a cookie, or a string of popcorn from the tree."

Adaline Karber's Christmas Tree Bread

A spectacular centerpiece that's easy to make and serve. Mrs. Karber, who professionally caters receptions, frequently offers this festive tree for holiday breakfasts.

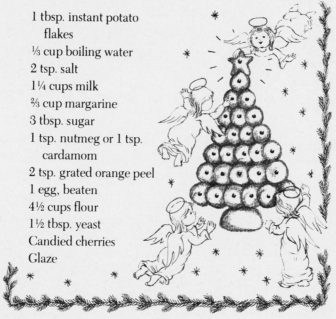

1 tbsp. instant potato
    flakes
⅓ cup boiling water
2 tsp. salt
1¼ cups milk
⅔ cup margarine
3 tbsp. sugar
1 tsp. nutmeg or 1 tsp.
    cardamom
2 tsp. grated orange peel
1 egg, beaten
4½ cups flour
1½ tbsp. yeast
Candied cherries
Glaze

Combine potato, boiling water, and salt, and mix as for mashed potatoes. Scald milk; add margarine, sugar, spice. Cool to luke-warm and combine with potato. Add orange peel and egg and mix. Gradually add 2 cups sifted flour and yeast to milk mixture. Beat until smooth. Cover and set in warm place for 10 minutes. Gradually add remaining flour. Turn onto lightly floured board and knead until smooth and elastic, about 8-10 minutes. Place in greased bowl, turning to grease top of dough. Cover with plastic wrap and set in warm place until doubled in bulk. Punch down.

On lightly floured board, roll dough out to ½-inch thickness. Cut 26 circles with 2-inch cookie cutter and 1 star. Reserve small piece of dough to make a tree base. Line 12×15-inch baking sheet with parchment. To begin tree, place 6 circles in a row, *overlapping slightly.* Lay 5 circles twice to form rows above, then 4, then 3, 2, 1, always overlapping. Place star on top. Press out base for tree to 5×2½×3 inches and place under bottom row. Place ½ candied cherry in center of each circle. Cover and let rise in warm place 15-20 minutes. Do not let rise to double. Brush with 1 egg beaten with 1 tbsp. water. Bake at 350° for 25 minutes or until golden brown. Brush with egg wash once more. Brush with 1 cup white Karo syrup brought to boiling point. Cool on rack. (Use leftover dough to make a few dinner rolls.)

17

Festive Apricot Braid

A delicate coffee bread, braided over a colorful filling of apricots and maraschino cherries makes this a royal offering for holiday guests.

¾ cup milk
⅓ cup butter or
    margarine
½ cup sugar
1 tsp. salt
1 pkg. active dry yeast
¼ cup lukewarm water
1 tsp. sugar
3 eggs
1 tsp. grated lemon peel
4¼-4½ cups flour
Apricot/Cherry Filling

In a saucepan combine milk and butter over medium heat until very warm. Stir in sugar and salt. Cool to lukewarm. Sprinkle yeast over water and sugar. Beat eggs in mixer bowl. Add lukewarm milk/butter mixture, yeast, and lemon peel. Gradually add 2 cups sifted flour and beat 5 minutes with electric mixer.

Gradually add 2 cups flour. Turn out onto lightly floured board and knead until smooth and elastic, 8-10 minutes, using extra flour as necessary. Place in greased bowl, turning to grease top of dough. Cover with plastic wrap and let rise in warm place until doubled in bulk. Prepare Apricot/Cherry Filling.

Punch dough down. Turn out onto lightly floured board and knead lightly. Divide dough in half. Roll one piece into an 8×14-inch rectangle. Transfer to greased baking sheet. Spread ½ prepared filling down center third of rectangle. Cut 1-inch-wide strips along both sides of filling, cutting from filling to outer edges of dough. Fold strips at an angle, crisscross, over filling. Repeat with remaining dough. Cover with kitchen towel and let rise in warm place until doubled in size. Brush with 1 egg beaten with 1 tsp. water. Bake at 375° for 20-25 minutes or until golden brown. Cool. Drizzle with icing.

Apricot/Cherry Filling: Combine 2½ cups (11 oz. package) chopped, dried apricots and 1½ cups water in saucepan. Bring to a boil; cook until all liquid is absorbed. Stir in ¾ cup packed brown sugar. Cool. Add 1 cup finely chopped, well-drained maraschino cherries and ½ cup chopped blanched almonds or walnuts. (Variation: Add ½ cup well-drained crushed pineapple.)

Icing: 1 cup powdered sugar, 1½ tbsp. hot water, 2-3 drops almond extract.

Christmas Breakfast Wreath

Red and green cherries, raisins, and nuts lend a decorative look to this holiday wreath.

½ cup milk	¼ cup lukewarm water
¼ cup butter	1 tsp. sugar
¼ cup sugar	3 eggs
1 tsp. salt	¼ tsp. cardamom
1 pkg. active dry yeast	3½-4 cups flour

In a saucepan over medium heat combine milk, butter, sugar, and salt until very warm. Cool to lukewarm. Sprinkle yeast over lukewarm water and sugar. Beat eggs in mixer bowl. Add cardamom, yeast, and milk/butter mixture. Gradually add 2 cups sifted flour and beat 5 minutes with electric mixer. Gradually add 1½ cups flour and turn out onto lightly floured board and knead until smooth and elastic, about 8-10 minutes. Add flour as necessary to prevent sticking. Place in greased bowl, turning to grease top of dough. Cover with plastic wrap and set in warm place until doubled in bulk.

Punch dough down and turn onto lightly floured board. Roll dough into a 10×30-inch rectangle. Sprinkle filling over dough, leaving a 1-inch edge. Roll dough up tightly from long end.

Seal edges and ends. With a knife, cut roll in half lengthwise. Turn cut sides up. Loosely braid ropes, keeping cut sides up. Transfer to greased baking sheet. Shape into 12-inch circle. Pinch ends together securely. Let rise in warm place until doubled in size. Brush with butter. Bake at 375° about 20 minutes or until golden brown. Cool. Drizzle with glaze of 1 cup powdered sugar, 2 tsp. each lemon juice and milk.

Filling: Beat together ¼ cup *each* butter and flour, 2 tbsp. sugar, ¼ cup almond paste, 1 tsp. grated lemon peel, ½ tsp. almond extract. Stir in ⅔ cup finely chopped blanched almonds, ¼ cup *each* red and green chopped candied cherries, ⅓ cup golden raisins.

Abundantly Alsatian

A visit to Marthe Nussbaumer's Alsatian home, Schweighof, is certain to include a gastronomic feast. In her spacious, sunny farm kitchen she combines a blend of French and German cuisines in her own creative Alsatian-style cooking. Baking is routine there, but at Christmas she deftly adds twenty different varieties of tiny, delicate cookies, a half-dozen breakfast braids, rolls, and a parade of elegant tortes and desserts. Her Christmas menus (opposite) deserve their own three-star awards.

Traditionally, the Nussbaumers share Christmas Eve supper and then a quiet, intimate Holy Evening with their family. It is a time of gratitude and reflection on the year's blessings. Even now, as young adults, the children present a program of French carols—singing, flute, piano—for their parents.

Marthe and husband, Roland, live on a large model farm in the picturesque rolling countryside near Altkirch. Hers is a busy life of homemaking, church activity, managing the large, old eighteen-room Nussbaumer family home, and extra weekend cooking for children and friends returning to Schweighof from work and study in the city. In summer Marthe raises a profusion of flowers, tends a vegetable garden, and frequently entertains tour groups visiting their farm.

Christmas Eve Supper at Schweighof

Crudités

Marinated Carrots, Beets,
Celery Root, French Green Beans,
Tomatoes & Onions

Winter Nüssli Salad
Vinaigrette Dressing

Baked Ham in Pastry Casing

Variety of French Provincial Cheeses
Crusty French Bread

Flaming "Norwegian Omlette"
(Baked Alaska Torte)
Christmas Cookies

Coffee with Whipped Cream

Christmas Day Dinner at Schweighof

Les Croûtes aux Morilles

Riesling d'Alsace

Lapin Rôti au Four a la Mode du Chef
Sauce au Riesling

Knöpfli
Salade Verte (Doucette) à la Vinaigrette

Glace à la Vanille Maison
Framboises Chaudes à la Liqueur

Bûche de Noël

Rumtopf

Petits Fours Maison
Café-Crème Chantilly

Breakfast Braid (Zopf)

The perfect combination with butter and homemade jam, this high, golden braid is baked both in Alsace and Switzerland. Erika Nussbaumer, Basel, shares her recipe.

1 cup milk	¼ cup lukewarm water
5 tbsp. butter	1 tsp. sugar
1 tsp. salt	4 cups flour
1 pkg. active dry yeast	Egg Glaze

In a saucepan combine milk, butter, and salt over medium heat until very warm. Cool to lukewarm. Dissolve yeast in water and sugar. Combine yeast and milk/butter mixture in mixer bowl. Gradually add 2 cups sifted flour and beat 5 minutes with electric mixer. Gradually add remaining flour. Turn out onto floured board and knead until smooth and elastic, about 8-10 minutes. Place in greased bowl, turning to grease top of dough. Cover with plastic wrap and set in warm place until doubled in bulk. Punch down. Divide into 3 equal pieces. Roll each piece into a 20-inch rope and braid, pinching ends together. Place on greased baking sheet. Cover with kitchen towel and set in warm place until almost doubled in size. Brush with 1 egg beaten with 1 tsp. water. Bake at 400° for 15 minutes. Reduce heat to 350° for another 15 minutes or until bread is hollow sounding when tapped. Cool on rack and cover with towel to soften. Makes 1 braid.

Austrians deck the halls—and all the other rooms—with boughs of evergreen. Before Christmas, living-room doors remain locked, sometimes for days. It is an old tradition that angels work inside, preparing for the coming of the Holy Child who brings the Christmas tree with all the candles and gifts spread below its branches.

A TINY SILVER BELL tinkled outside the Trapp family's living room—the signal that the long-awaited moment, Christmas Eve, had arrived. Brimming with excitement, the children rushed down the long staircase of their Tyrolean home to the large festive parlor where, for the first time, they saw their Christmas tree, bright with more than a hundred lighted candles. It was the youngest of the children who came forward and recited, from memory, the Christmas story from the Bible. Then a hushed singing of "Stille Nacht" (Silent Night)," handshakes, hugs, kisses, and many a wish for "a blessed Christmas."

After supper and hasty naps, Baron Von Trapp, the first to awaken, stood with lantern in hand at the foot of the dark stairway, beckoning his children in song:

> *Shepherds quickly waken from your sleep,*
> *The Good Shepherd is now awake.*

From the top of the stairs they came in procession, each child carrying a flickering lantern and singing. Gathered below, they formed a choir:

> *Hurry, oh hurry and gifts you bring;*
> *Come and adore Him, the Little King.*

Then it was off to church with lanterns lighting the dark, snowy path as they joined their neighbors in a joyous midnight celebration.

CZECH FARMERS gladly share part of the Christmas Eve meal with their faithful animals. Even bees and fruit trees may be given special offerings of food and drink—in hope of a good harvest. All that lives and grows on the farm must share in this meal to ensure prosperity in the coming year.

Czechoslovakian Vánočka

A delectable breakfast or dessert bread for the Christmas holidays. The Czechs call it Van-*och*-ka.

¾ cup milk
½ cup sweet butter
⅔ cup sugar
1 tsp. salt
2 pkg. active dry yeast
½ cup lukewarm water
2 tsp. sugar

3 egg yolks
Grated peel of ½ lemon
4-4½ cups flour
¾ cup golden raisins
½ cup chopped blanched almonds
Egg Glaze
Sliced almonds

Combine milk and butter over medium heat until very warm. Stir in sugar and salt. Sprinkle yeast over water and sugar and dissolve. Beat egg yolks in mixer bowl; add lemon peel, yeast, and milk/butter mixtures. Gradually add 2 cups sifted flour and beat 5 minutes with electric mixer. Gradually add 2 cups flour and turn out onto lightly floured board. Use additional flour as necessary. Knead until smooth and elastic, about 8-10 minutes. Work in raisins and almonds evenly. Place in greased bowl, turning to grease top of dough. Cover with plastic wrap and set in warm place until doubled in bulk. Punch down.

Divide dough in half. Cut first half in 3 equal pieces. Cut remaining half in 4 equal pieces. Allow dough to rest 10 minutes. Roll 3 largest pieces into 18-inch rolls. Braid and pinch ends together. Place on greased baking sheet.

Roll 3 of the smaller pieces to 16-inch rolls and braid. Pinch ends together and place smaller braid on top of larger braid. Take remaining single portion of dough and divide in half. Roll into 2 18-inch strips. Twist strips together, rope-style. Place twist on top of smaller braid, tucking ends under larger braid. Cover and let rise in warm place until almost doubled in size. Brush with 1 egg slightly beaten with 1 tsp. water. Sprinkle with sliced almonds. Bake at 350° 35-40 minutes or until bread is hollow sounding on bottom when tapped. Cool.

Vánočka may also be iced with ¾ cup sifted powdered sugar, 2-3 tsp. milk, ⅛ tsp. almond extract. If icing, retain sliced almonds for sprinkling over frosting.

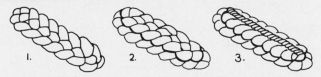

In Czechoslovakia, Christmas Eve is known as Štědrý Večer—the very rich night—because there are so many gifts and good things to eat.

TIP: "When stacking braided breads, do NOT put any butter or oil on the braids. Stand over the loaf(ves) when stacking, being sure to place each loaf directly on top each other. If not squarely centered, pick it up and move it until it is," says bread baking instructor, Sam Kirk. "If loaves slip during oven rise (watch carefully during the first five minutes of baking), then open the oven door, take out the baking sheet, and without hesitation, move the loaf(ves) around until it/they are centered again."

YOUR FUTURE IN A NUTSHELL. According to a quaint Czech tradition, young people play fortunetelling games on Christmas Eve. They simply float a nutshell with a lighted candle in a tub of water. If the shell moves toward the center of the tub, the owner goes on a trip. If the shell hovers near the rim, there's no journey in store. Should two shells float toward each other? A wedding's in the offing. Floating away—there's a year's delay.

"CRISPY APPLE STRUDEL, cookies, and a variety of Christmas rolls filled Mother's large cut-glass tray on Christmas Eve," remembers Lubuska Jerebek of her childhood in Prague. "The tray was left on the table for nibbling and quickly refilled when guests arrived."

For superstitious reasons, Mother never served "meat with feathers" for our Christmas meal. She maintained our good luck might fly away!

In our house there was a lot of singing. We children performed for our parents with guitar and piano. Most of the songs were spontaneous, with Mother starting a carol and everyone chiming in.

31

Dutch New Year's Olliebollen

This version of *Olliebollen* (sometimes called *Olykoeks*) allows you to serve fresh, warm fritters for a New Year's Day breakfast.

⅓ cup lukewarm milk
1 pkg. active dry yeast
¼ cup lukewarm water
1 tsp. sugar
1 egg

1 tsp. salt
2¼ cups flour
1½ cups raisins and
    currants
1 tart apple, chopped

Heat milk to lukewarm. Dissolve yeast in water and sugar. Beat egg in mixer bowl. Add salt, yeast mixture, and milk. Gradually add sifted flour. Beat about 5 minutes with electric mixer. Add raisins and apple. Cover bowl with plastic wrap. Let stand overnight in refrigerator. (Or let rise until doubled and bake immediately.) Next morning, let stand in warm place to finish rising. In an electric skillet or deep fat fryer, heat cooking oil to 375°. With 2 iced teaspoons, shape small portions of batter into balls. Turn when golden brown. Drain on paper towels. Roll in sugar. Serve warm.

Tip: Chill spoons overnight in freezer.

When Johanna Hekkert, Sunnyvale, California, makes *Ollie-bollen* on New Year's Day, she makes *Appelflappen* at the same time. Apple slices, dipped in egg batter, are fried to golden perfection, sprinkled with sugar, and eaten as fast as she can fry them.

o   o   o

Among the early Dutch settlers in New York State's Hudson Valley it was customary to hold open house on New Year's Day. Good food (including *Olliebollen*) and good fellowship abounded.

Young men were known to rush from house to house, challenging each other to see who could make the most calls—especially where there were young ladies. A measure of a girl's popularity depended on the number of eligible young bachelors on the guest list. Eventually Dutch families took out newspaper ads announcing the hours during which they would receive callers on that day.

THE NÜRNBERG CHRISTKINDLESMARKT (Christ Child's Market) is thought to be the oldest Christmas fair in Germany. Its 400-year-old tradition, charming decorations, and myriads of lights in the old city all blend together in a captivating atmosphere for thousands of visitors. The market is really its own little town, spreading over the cobblestone square between the *Frauenkirche* (Church of Our Lady) and the beautiful old fountain, *Schöne Brunnen.*

More than 200 red-striped, canopied stalls offer a dazzling array of things to celebrate—the tiniest of handmade ornaments . . . wooden soldier nutcrackers . . . old-fashioned prune dolls. Vendors beckon you to sample their juicy *Bratwurst* and crunchy rolls. Burnt almonds . . . mountains of Fruit Bread . . . heaps of freshly baked *Lebkuchen* (honey cookies) . . . marzipan candies . . . all tempt you from stall to stall.

There a shepherds' choir plays from the steps of the *Frauenkirche.* . . . At the bakery corner an organ grinder in a red St. Nicholas suit cranks out "O Tannenbaum. . . ." For the children, there is a puppet theater . . . for adults, organ concerts and Christmas oratorios in the church.

The ancient crafts of skilled Nürnberg artists . . . the lovely Christmas music . . . the delicious—but crazy—mixture of foods . . . all make this market an exciting December adventure.

Traditional Früchtebrot/Kletzenbrot

(Fruit Bread)

Kletze (*Klay*-tze), a word used by farmers, means pear. Known also as *Hutzelbrot* and *Birnenbrot* (pear bread), this old German favorite is laden with moist dried fruits and nuts. Hundreds of loaves of Fruit Bread are sold daily at the Nürnberg Christ Child's Market during the Advent season. Lilly Gyger, Füllinsdorf, Switzerland, shares a very old family recipe.

1 cup (6 oz.) dried
   pears, halved
¾ cup pitted prunes,
   coarsely chopped
1 cup golden raisins
1 cup dark raisins
¾ cup figs, halved
½ cup whole almonds
1¼ cups walnut halves
¾ cup whole filberts
¾ cup candied orange
   peel
2 tbsp. vanilla°

2 tbsp. lemon juice
2 tbsp. grated lemon peel

Bread Dough
¾ cup milk
½ cup sweet butter
2 tbsp. active dry yeast
¼ cup lukewarm water
1 tbsp. sugar
1 tsp. salt
1 tsp. *each* coriander,
   mace, ground anise seed
2 cups flour

Cover pears with water and cook slightly. (Do not overcook or pears become mushy.) Drain. Cool. Pat dry. Cover prunes with hot water and allow to stand briefly. Cool. Drain and pat dry. Wash and dry raisins. Combine all remaining fruits and nuts in large bowl. Sprinkle with vanilla, lemon juice, and peel. °(European bakers sprinkle fruit with 2 tbsp. *Kirschwasser*.) Let fruit stand while preparing bread dough, or for several hours. Stir fruit occasionally.

In a saucepan combine milk and butter over medium heat until very hot. Cool to lukewarm. Sprinkle yeast over water and sugar to dissolve. Combine milk/butter and yeast mixtures; add salt and spices. Gradually work in sifted flour and beat 5 minutes with electric mixer. Cover with plastic wrap and set in warm place until doubled in bulk. Punch dough down.

Knead dough into bowl of fruit, distributing evenly. Spoon into 2 well-greased 4½×7½-inch loaf pans. Cover and let rise in warm place until doubled in size, about 2-3 hours. Brush with water. Garnish with blanched almond halves and candied cherries. Bake at 325° 1 hour or until done. Brush with water several times while baking. Remove from pans and cool. Wrap in aluminum foil. Age at least 1 week before slicing. Fruit Bread improves greatly with age. Serve with butter.

This bread looks rather "rough" and plain. It may be glazed or brushed with white Karo syrup while still warm.

Mother used to dry fruits from the garden down in the lower basement, remembers Margaret Kulish of her childhood home in Austria. Bunches of grapes were cut fresh from the vine in the late summer afternoon when they had cooled from the heat of the sun. Dried on the stem, they were sweet as plums. Apple slices, succulent with sugar, were strung like beads on white thread to dry for winter baking. We also had pears. Mother's fruit had a lovely aroma and a very distinct flavor I don't find in commercially dried fruits.

o   o   o

German farm women dried their orchard fruit in big outdoor ovens after bread baking. Later it was stored in baskets in the attic. Choicest dried pears, grapes, and plums they saved for the Christmas Fruit Bread/*Kletzenbrot*.

o   o   o

Austrian women used knitting needles to poke holes in the *Kletzenbrot* (pear bread)—then poured in *Mirabella Schnaps* (yellow plum liqueur) for extra flavor and good keeping.

Bunte Teller

The custom of Bunte Teller, a brightly colored dish laden with fruit, nuts, and homebaked cookies, originated in Germany.

Early on Christmas Eve, Mother covered the table with her best cloth and we children set out special deep plates to be filled with nuts and candies. My plate, white with a deep pink fluted edge, came from Russia.... Later we went to bed and tried hard to sleep, but couldn't. In the stillness we'd hear a clink, clink, clink from the dining room. This was Dad, putting the peanuts, nuts, and candies on our plates. Beside the plate they put a little gift. One in particular I remember—a little purse with a tiny mirror in the lid. All my friends at church envied me on Christmas morning. (Bertha Fast Harder is a Christian education instructor in Elkhart, Indiana.)

German Christstollen

The baking of Christmas *Stollen* is another ancient German custom, orignating in Dresden about 1400. In those days people tried to represent biblical ideas in baking. Many old cookie forms and molds depict familiar Bible stories. The *Stollen* form represents the Christ Child in swaddling clothes.

Stollen is traditionally rich in butter, raisins, almonds, and citron; the top is generously dusted with confectioners' sugar. This bread is served in every German home at Christmas.

¾ cup golden raisins
½ cup dark raisins
¼ cup currants
½ cup blanched slivered
    almonds, lightly toasted
¾ cup candied orange
    peel
½ cup + 1 tbsp.
    lukewarm milk
¼ cup sugar

2 pkg. active dry yeast
4 cups flour
2 eggs
1 vanilla bean or 2 tbsp.
    vanilla
Granted rind of 1 lemon
½ tsp. mace
⅛ tsp. cardamom
1 tsp. almond extract
¼ tsp. salt
1 cup sweet butter

Prepare fruit and nuts in a bowl. (Optional: Sprinkle with ¼ cup rum or brandy and mix well. Let stand 1 hour. Drain fruit on paper towel and press dry.) Sprinkle with ¼ cup of the flour and toss.

Place warm milk, 2 tbsp. sugar, and yeast in a bowl. Beat in 1 cup sifted flour. Cover and let rise in warm place 20 minutes. Beat eggs and remaining sugar. Add vanilla bean seeds or vanilla extract, lemon peel, salt, cardamom, mace, and almond extract and mix well. Add sponge and mix. Gradually add 1 cup flour and beat 5 minutes with electric mixer or knead by hand until smooth and elastic. Cover with plastic wrap and set in warm place 15 minutes. *(Please turn page.)*

Margaret Kulish says it was traditional in Austria to make the motion of the cross three times with the knife before cutting the Stollen.

Combine remaining flour and butter as for pie crust. Knead into firm ball. Combine yeast dough and flour/butter dough. On lightly floured board knead the combined doughs until smooth and elastic. Cover with plastic wrap and let stand in warm place until doubled in bulk. Punch dough down. Gently knead in fruit and nuts, a small amount at a time, working carefully so as not to discolor dough; distribute fruit evenly. Divide dough in half. Lightly roll and pat dough to 8×12-inch oval. Brush with melted butter. Turn dough over lengthwise and seal in typical *Stollen* form (see picture). Repeat with remaining dough. Place *Stollen* on parchment-lined baking tins. Cover and let rise until doubled in size. (This is slow; allow enough time.) Brush each *Stollen* well with melted butter. Bake at 350° about 45 minutes or until hollow sounding when tapped with your knuckles. While warm, brush again with melted butter. Dust generously with sifted powdered sugar. Cool. Wrap in aluminum foil and store in a cool place to mellow for a week. Cut in thin slices and serve with sweet butter. *Stollen* lasts a long time if securely wrapped in foil in the refrigerator. (If making 1 large *Stollen*, bake for 60 minutes.)

"*Christstollen* is lighter than *Dresdenerstollen*," explains Masterbaker, Karl Kaestel, Nürnberg. "Both are rich in almonds, fruit, and spices," he says, "but it is the *zitronat* (citron) that gives the *Stollen* its 'certain joy.'"

Fatschen, the old German word meaning to wrap or bind, is still used in some parts of South Germany and Austria, says Elisabeth Mödlhammer. Earlier *Fatschenkinder*, made of wax or silver, were used as votive offerings. Baked as molded cookies or cakes, they were given as gifts to new mothers (a kind of "good health" greeting) and as wedding gifts, wishing the bride and groom to be richly blessed with children.

In the last bread baking before Christmas, Bavarian farm women used their better flour to make a *Christkindl* or *Fatschenkindl* to serve for a pre-Christmas meal. *Fatschenkinder*, baked in this ancient, simple form, still remind us of the infant Jesus, "wrapped in swaddling clothes and laid in a manger."

South German Fatschenkind

The world-famous Dallmeyer Delicatessen, Munich, Germany, has served kings and princes with a wide array of house specialties, exotic fruits from distant lands, and baking delights. One of their Christmas bakery offerings is the *Fatschenkind* (or *Wickelkind*), a breakfast bread shaped like a babe in swaddling clothes. Germans have baked cookies, cakes, or bread in this form since the 1600s.

¾ cup milk
⅓ cup butter
⅓ cup sugar
1 tsp. salt
1 pkg. active dry yeast

¼ cup lukewarm water
1 tsp. sugar
1 egg
4-4½ cups flour
Egg Glaze
Currants or raisins

Heat milk and butter until very warm. Add sugar and salt and mix. Cool to lukewarm. Dissolve yeast in water with sugar. Beat egg in mixer bowl. Add yeast and milk/butter mixtures. Gradually add 2 cups sifted flour and beat 5 minutes with electric mixer. Gradually add remaining 2 cups sifted flour.

44

Turn out onto lightly floured board and knead until smooth and elastic, about 8-10 minutes. Dough should not stick to the board. Place in greased bowl, turning to grease top of dough. Cover with plastic wrap and set in warm place until doubled in bulk. Punch dough down.

Small Fatschenkinder: Divide dough into 6 equal parts. (Cut a tiny piece of dough from each for decoration.) Roll each piece into a smooth 8-inch oblong. With the side of your hand, "cut" a head for each body, leaving it slightly attached to body (see p. 89, 1 and 2). Place *Fatschenkinder* on greased baking sheets. Flatten bodies and shape (see picture, p. 43). Cover with kitchen towel and let rise in warm place for 15 minutes. Meanwhile, add a little extra flour to each remaining piece of dough. Roll out into very long, thin strips for decoration. Brush each "child" with 1 egg beaten with 1 tsp. water. Lay decorative strip on "child" as illustrated on page 43. Brush strip with egg. Punch currants or raisins into each body for eyes, nose, and button decor. Let rise until doubled in bulk. Bake at 350° for 15-17 minutes or until hollow-sounding when tapped. Cool on rack and cover with towel to soften. Makes 6 *Fatschenkinder.*

Large Fatschenkind: Use entire piece of dough to make 1 large "child." Follow directions as above. Use whole blanched almonds for decoration.

Greek Advent Eftazymo

Efta in Greek means "seven." *Zymo*—knead. Bread kneaded seven times—that's *Eftazymo!*

Made during the Advent season, this pre-Christmas bread depends on an interesting combination of chick peas and wood ashes for leavening. The night before baking, Greek women grind chick peas, add salt, a sprinkling of wood ash, and hot water to a large pot. This is covered and set in a warm place to ferment overnight.

In the morning, foam from the peas is skimmed off and mixed with a half cup of flour and placed in a warm, sunny spot to rise. (If there is no foam, start the whole process again!) Foam and flour are added to the starter two more times; finally sugar, egg, anise, and remaining flour are added to make a dough.

Baked to a crusty golden brown, this bread of "seven kneadings" is a lot of work. But Greeks insist the flavor and aroma of *Eftazymo* are worth all the effort. For curious readers, here are the (untested) ingredients: 8 oz. chick peas, ½ tsp. salt, ½ tsp. wood ashes, 1¼ cups hot water, 9½ cups flour, 1 tsp. ground anise seed, ½ cup sugar, 1 egg, water to make soft dough. Yield: 2 large loaves.

"*CHRISTMAS IN OUR GREEK VILLAGE* had a special 'flavor,'" recalls Kristina Scamagus of San Jose, California. "There was heart and spirit in the celebration. Even though times were difficult and people worked very hard, I remember their smiling faces had real peace and joy."

Kristina's mother still bakes their traditional Christmas bread, *Christopsomo*. In her village families were large and on farms there were extra workers to cook for, so women baked from ten to twelve big loaves of *Christopsomo* at one time. "It was a lot of work, making the fire and heating up the big outdoor oven. You had to wait a long time for the temperature to be just right."

Greeks traditionally top *Christopsomo* with a cross. To this Kristina's mother adds birds, daisies, and flowers, all sculptured out of bread dough. "The bread was placed in the center of the table because the ladies were proud of their cheerful decorations."

𝕲𝖗𝖊𝖊𝖐 𝕮𝖍𝖗𝖎𝖘𝖙𝖔𝖕𝖘𝖔𝖒𝖔

(Christmas Bread)

Walnut halves and a cross decorate this ancient Christmas bread from Greece. The special flavoring is *masticha*.

½ cup milk
1 cup butter
⅔ cup sugar
1 tsp. salt
1-1½ tbsp. *masticha*°
    or 2 tsp. crushed
    anise seed
2 pkg. active dry yeast
½ cup lukewarm water
1 tsp. sugar
4 eggs
5½-6 cups flour

Pulverize masticha in blender or crush anise seeds with mortar and pestle. Combine milk, sugar, salt, butter, and *masticha* (or anise) and bring to a boil. Cool to lukewarm. Sprinkle yeast

---

°*Masticha* or gum mastic is a resin from the Mediterranean mastic tree, available in Middle Eastern delis and markets.

48

over water and 1 tsp. sugar and dissolve. Combine with luke-warm milk/butter mixture. Beat eggs in mixer bowl and add the milk/yeast mixture. Gradually add 1½ cups sifted flour to liquid. Beat 2 minutes with electric mixer. Gradually add 4 cups flour. turn out onto lightly floured board and knead until smooth and elastic, about 8-10 minutes, adding last ½ cup flour as necessary. Place in greased bowl, turning to grease top of dough. Cover with plastic wrap and set in warm place until doubled in bulk. Punch down.

Turn dough onto floured board and knead lightly. Pinch off 2 pieces of dough, each about 3 inches in diameter. Set aside. Shape remaining dough into a round loaf, and place pucker side down on greased baking sheet. Flatten with palm of hand. Roll each of the small balls into 14-inch ropes. cut a 5-inch slash at the end of each. Lay ropes on loaf, crossing ropes at center of loaf. Curl slashed ends away from the center, forming a small circle. Place walnut half in each circle and one in center of cross. Cover and let rise until doubled in size. Brush with slightly beaten egg white. (Optional: sprinkle with sesame seeds.) Bake at 350° for 45 minutes or until hollow sounding when tapped. Cool. Makes 1 large loaf.

Before cutting this loaf, the Greek father makes the sign of the cross with a knife and wishes everyone joy and health.

"*DECEMBER 6* is the beginning of our Christmas season in Hungary," says Iren Romoda. "On that day Mother often planted little plates of wheat seed which grew to about an inch and a half. The bright green was very nice when everything was gray and dreary outdoors. Sometimes she used it as the centerpiece for our Christmas dinner." (The memory of the wheat prompted Mrs. Romoda to revive this old tradition with her own family.)

"In South Hungary it was traditional to bring wheat straw into the house, spreading it around the room. Our mother never allowed us to do that; she thought it much too messy. But we children loved to play in it at the neighbors. Sometimes their presents got lost in the straw.

"Our big pastry in Hungary—and all the Slavic countries—is poppy seed roll. You're offered this treat wherever you go. We Hungarians joke about 'getting roll poisoning.' We also ate a lot of dried fruits during the holidays. Hard candies were made at home and wrapped in colored foil to hang on the tree. There was a lot of scrambling for those candies when the tree came down on January 6.

"Christmas Eve celebrations are very private. There are no presents—just a tree, candle, and much singing." (Mrs. Romoda teaches Slavic languages in Berkeley, California.)

MERRY CHRISTMAS! Say it with food. A loaf of sweet bread to a new neighbor. A plate of cookies for a lonely child. A cake says more than a handclasp. A recipe shared with a new friend is a link forever. These warm, human, get-to-know-you better gifts of love show that you care. Know someone who needs a lift? Say Merry Christmas—with a gift from your kitchen.

Hungarian Diós Kalács

(Walnut Roll)

Typical of Old World recipes is this walnut roll (*dee*-ohsh *kah*-lahch) brought to this country by grandmothers of Hungarian, Yugoslav, Croatian, and Russian backgrounds. A Slavic holiday favorite, the rich coffee bread is enhanced by a filling of ground nuts, honey, and raisins.

Dough
2 pkg. active dry yeast
½ cup lukewarm milk
2 tsp. sugar
¼ cup butter
½ cup sugar
½ tsp. salt
2 egg yolks
1 whole egg
½ cup sour cream
3½-4 cups flour

Walnut Filling
¼ cup butter
1 cup sugar
½ cup heavy cream
¼ cup honey
1 tsp. vanilla
3½ cups ground walnuts
1 tsp. cinnamon
1 cup golden raisins
Melted butter

Sprinkle yeast over warm milk and 2 tsp. sugar. Heat sour cream over low heat just to lukewarm. Cream butter and sugar; add eggs and beat well. Add warm sour cream, yeast, salt, and mix. Gradually add 1½ cups sifted flour. Beat 5 minutes with electric mixer. Gradually add 2 cups sifted flour. Turn out onto lightly floured board and knead until smooth and elastic, about 8-10 minutes. Use additional flour to keep dough from sticking. Place in greased bowl, turning to grease top of dough. Cover with plastic wrap and set in warm place until doubled in bulk.

Punch dough down, working out air bubbles. Divide dough in half. On lightly floured board, roll half of dough into a 12×12-inch square. Spread half of filling over dough to within 1 inch of edge. Sprinkle with half the cinnamon and raisins. Roll as for jelly roll. Pinch ends and seam together and turn under. Place seam side down on greased baking sheet. Repeat with remaining dough. Prick top of roll every 3 inches with fork to eliminate air bubbles. Brush with melted butter. Cover with kitchen towel and set in warm place to rise until doubled in size. Bake at 350° for 35-40 minutes or until done. If necessary, cover lightly with foil to prevent burning. Brush again with melted butter. Cool on wire rack. Wrap in foil. Freezes well. Makes 2 loaves. *(Please turn page.)*

Walnut Roll Filling: Plump raisins in hot water. Drain and pat dry. In a saucepan on low burner, melt butter. Stir in sugar, cream, honey, and bring to a boil. Add vanilla and walnuts. Cool. If filling is too thick to spread, add a little extra cream or milk.

Eithne Cuckel's father, Mayo County, Ireland, called Christmas Eve the night of the "Big Nuff"—the one night everyone had enough to eat.

Mary Sheridan's Irish Soda Bread

Mary's mother, Bridget Kelly, brought this recipe from Ireland where they baked soda bread in iron skillets on the open hearth. Mary still skillet-bakes the bread as regular fare for her family and presents it as gifts on holidays to friends in Santa Clara, California.

5 cups flour	1-¾ cups raisins
1 tsp. soda	1½ tsp. caraway
1½ tsp. baking powder	2 tsp. grated orange
1 cup sugar	peel (optional)
1 cup butter	1 egg, slightly beaten
	2½ cups buttermilk

Sift dry ingredients together. (You may use ½ whole wheat flour if desired.) Cut butter in small pieces and work into flour with your hands. Add raisins, caraway seed, and orange rind. Beat egg lightly; add buttermilk and pour into dry mixture. Mix well. Pour batter into large greased cast iron skillet or dutch oven; form into round ball. With a sharp knife, cut a cross in the center top. Bake at 350° for 60-75 minutes or until knife inserted in center comes out clean. Cool. Allow to stand 1 day before cutting.

Poems, Promises, & Presepe

When I was a schoolgirl in Naples, Italy, we wrote Christmas letters full of promises to our parents, relates Matilde Oliverio. Though this happened yearly, Father still expressed great surprise each time he "discovered" our epistles hidden under his napkin or plate at the dinner table. It was also customary for us to recite long, beautiful poems to our parents before dessert (*panettone, torrone, struffoli . . .*) was served. Eel is the traditional meat for an Italian Christmas Eve. Chestnuts, too, are part of the meal—and many sweets.

In Italy the Christmas celebration centers around the *presepe* (crèche) with all its figures—often family heirlooms. We had family prayers around our *presepe* each morning.

There is a lovely candle ceremony practiced in some of our Italian villages: At the Christmas dinner the father lights a candle and passes it down through the family members until it reaches the youngest. If there is a baby, the mother holds the candle in the baby's hand and together they put it in the center of the table. If there is no baby, they blow it out and save it for next year's Christmas, hoping by then there will be a new baby! (Mrs. Oliverio shares holiday traditions in her Italian language classes in San Jose, California.)

Panettone

A light cake-bread eaten throughout Italy, especially at Christmas, with breakfast coffee. Legend tells that this fruity bread was created in Milan. In order to win the hand of the girl he loved, a young nobleman named Antonio hired himself to the girl's father, a baker. To make an impression and improve a waning business, Toni added butter and sugar to the bread dough, tossed in candied fruits and several dozen eggs. People liked his bread which became known as "Pane di Toni," or Toni's bread.

½ cup lukewarm milk
1 pkg. active dry yeast
¼ cup lukewarm water
1 tsp. sugar
¾ cup sweet butter
½ cup sugar
½ tsp. salt
5 egg yolks
1 whole egg

½ tsp. grated lemon peel
3½-4 cups flour
½ cup golden and dark
  raisins combined
½ cup blanched slivered
  almonds
¼ cup diced candied
  orange and lemon
  peel combined

(Optional: Plump raisins in a little brandy.) Heat milk to lukewarm. Dissolve yeast in warm water with sugar. Cream butter. Beat in sugar; add salt. Add egg yolks and whole egg, 1 at a time. Beat until smooth. Add 2 cups sifted flour. Beat 5 minutes with electric mixer. Stir in yeast, milk, and lemon peel. Gradually add remaining flour and turn out onto lightly floured board and knead until smooth, elastic, and no longer sticky, about 8-10 minutes. Gently work in raisins, almonds, and candied peel. Place in greased bowl, turning to grease top of dough. Cover with plastic wrap and let rise in warm place until doubled in bulk (about 3 hours).

Punch dough down. Turn onto lightly floured board and knead lightly. Divide in half. Shape into 2 round loaves about 6 inches in diameter. Place on greased baking sheet or in greased cake pans. Cover and let rise in warm place until doubled in size. Brush with melted butter or 1 egg beaten with 1 tsp. water. Cut cross in tops with sharp knife. Bake at 350° for 30 minutes or until golden brown. Cover with foil if necessary to prevent burning. Cool on wire rack. Slice and serve warm with butter.

LA BEFANA, a good little witch, was sweeping her house the night the wise men came by with presents for the Baby Jesus—so the legend goes. The kings invited the old woman to come with them to Bethlehem, but La Befana foolishly refused, saying she had work to do.

Later, broom still in hand, La Befana set out to catch up with them, but lost her way. She has never found the wise men, Bethlehem, or the *Bambino*. Every year she goes through Italy, searching, leaving presents for the good children on her way. Italian boys and girls eagerly await La Befana, writing letters and lists for their presents. On January 6 their stockings are filled—by La Befana.

Christmas Sleigh Rides

In Poland the days between Christmas and New Year were such merry, festive times. When I was a young girl there were moonlight sleigh rides with prancing horses and jingling bells.

Buried under lap robes and bundled in caps and mufflers, we sang and laughed our way from village to village. At least once during the evening, the driver made a sudden, sharp turn, dumping everyone into the cold, wet snow. A warm welcome— glowing hearth, honey cakes, and poppy seed rolls—awaited us at a friend's home where we sang and laughed some more.

During Christmas week people did as little work as possible, leaving plenty of time to celebrate, to enjoy their Christmas trees decked with apples, nuts, candies, hand-blown decorated eggs. There was a lot of visiting, eating, and singing. "Those times are among my fondest memories."—Shared by Wera Kawulka, who helps keep traditions alive in a South Bay (California) Polish Women's Organization.

A Polish Christmas Eve Supper

(Wigilia)

Pickled Herring in Sour Cream

Borscht without Meat

Pierogi—Cheese and Sauerkraut

Northern Pike

Fish and Horseradish Sauce

Pickled Beets

Noodles with Poppy Seed and Raisins

Poppy Seed Rolls

Christmas Bread

Light Fruitcake

Twelve Fruit Compote

Christmas Eve supper begins when the first star appears in the evening sky.

Polish Poppy Seed Roll

Before the Christmas Eve meal, Polish families share a communion wafer, *oplatek*, a symbol of love, friendship, and forgiveness. One does not come to Christmas without forgetting and forgiving. Our supper is not lavish, but includes traditional dishes, among which is poppy seed roll, says Wera Kawulka. An extra plate is set for a stranger—who might be Christ.

Dough

2 pkg. active dry yeast
¼ cup lukewarm water
2 tsp. sugar
¼ cup butter
½ cup sugar
2 egg yolks
1 whole egg
1 cup lukewarm sour cream
½ tsp. salt
4-4½ cups flour
Egg Glaze

Poppy Seed Filling

2 cups poppy seeds
½ cup boiling milk
¾ cup sugar
2 tbsp. butter
2 tbsp. heavy cream
3 tbsp. honey
2 tsp. grated orange peel
2 egg whites
1 tart apple, grated, or
    ¼-½ cup golden raisins
    (optional)

Sprinkle yeast over warm water and sugar. Heat sour cream over low heat just until lukewarm. Cream butter and sugar; add eggs and beat well. Add warm sour cream, yeast, salt, and mix. Gradually add 1½ cups sifted flour. Beat 5 minutes with electric mixer. Gradually add 2½ cups sifted flour. Turn out onto lightly floured board and knead until smooth and elastic, about 8-10 minutes. Use additional flour to keep dough from sticking. Place in greased bowl, turning to grease top of dough. Cover with plastic wrap and set in warm place until double in bulk. Punch dough down. Cover and let rise in warm place again until double in bulk.

Punch dough down. Divide in half. On lightly floured board, roll half of dough to 14×14-inch square. Spread half of filling over dough to within 1 inch of edge. Sprinkle with grated apple or raisins (optional). Carefully roll as for jelly roll. Pinch ends and seam together and turn under. Place seam side down on greased baking sheet. Repeat with remaining dough. Cover with kitchen towel and set in warm place until doubled in size. Brush with 1 egg beaten with 1 tsp. water. Bake at 350° for 40 minutes or until done. If necessary, cover lightly with foil to prevent burning. Cool. Wrap in foil. Freezes well. Makes 2 loaves.

Filling: (Optional: Plump raisins or grated apple.) Cover poppy seeds with boiling milk; cover and let steam 30 minutes. Grind. Combine sugar, cream, honey, butter, peel, and poppy seeds. Bring to a boil and cook 5 minutes over low heat. Cool. Beat egg whites until stiff. Gently fold in poppy seeds.

A Finnish Country Christmas

We choose our Christmas tree in summer while gathering wild blueberries in the woods near our home. When someone spots a tree that is round, full, and just the right height he shouts, "There's our Christmas tree!" (In winter when the trees are laden with snow, it is difficult to see their shape.) The tree is carefully marked and then early on the morning of December 24, Father and the boys go out and cut it. When it's dry, we bring the tree indoors to decorate.

On Christmas Eve everyone eagerly waits for the visit from *Joulupukki* (you-lo-poh-kay), our Finnish Santa Claus. He's a jolly fellow in red fur-trimmed suit and shiny black boots. Making a big noise with his stick he calls, "Where are all the good and obedient children in this house?" Father invites him in, offering a chair. *Joulupukki* tells of his sleigh ride from Lapland, about his workshop and calls us to sit on his knee, inquiring if we've been good. We are a little scared, yet curious. He asks if we've helped Mother. Do we tease each other or the cat? Actually, he already knows all about us from his little helpers, the *Joulutontut*, who peek in windows before Christmas. For those who've been obedient and good, there are gifts in his bag. Sometimes we sing and dance with him around the tree.

Now it's time for some of us to clean up the paper and ribbons from his presents while the others go for a Christmas *sauna* (sow-na, as the Finns say). Then there's dinner and finally it's time to light candles on the tree. In Finland we add Christmas sparklers—like Americans use on the Fourth of July. Because the tree is so fresh, we can hang them right on the branches. What a lovely sight to see, candles and sparklers lighting the dark room.

On Christmas Eve Father gives the animals extra straw and lots of hay to munch all night. Before going to bed, my parents go to the barn to feed them once more and wish these, our animal friends, a Merry Christmas.

Church is at 7:00 the next morning, but we must be up at least by 4:30 since we have two hours to go by sleigh. The night is dark and cold; stars are still out. Gladly we snuggle under Mother's warm woolen comforter, embroidered and decorated with bright pom-poms.

Our parish is large, the church building very old (300 years) and there is no heat. Often we must stand, for the sanctuary is packed. Our usually conservative pastor celebrates this special day in a white robe with festive colors. Daylight is just breaking when the service is over. Another two hours by sleigh and we return to a breakfast of ham, fruit soup with dried plums and raisins, and Mother's Christmas *pulla* (p. 70).

For us Finns, Christmas is a very quiet day. Children play with new toys, parents read new books, or even take a nap, since we were up very early. Dinner is served in the afternoon.

On St. Stephens' Day (December 26) there is a special childrens' church service. It is a cheerful, lively day—a day for play.

(Memories shared by Terttu Pujanen Gilbert of her childhood in Finland. She now lives in California.)

FINNISH FARM WIVES traditionally are great bakers. Their old-time ovens were built into a wall behind the stove, like a tunnel, about three feet wide and sometimes six feet deep.

At baking time, a wood fire was lit in the oven. When it had burned down, the red, glowing embers were raked to the front of the stove with a kind of shovel on a long pole. The women then brushed out the oven with a wet broom. A ventilator at the back of the stove drew off the smoke while a damper regulated the heat.

Heating the oven was a lot of work, as was mixing and kneading large batches of dough by hand. Usually they baked for the entire week. Terttu Gilbert says their big wood-burning stove had to be heated for two hours before baking. "When the heat was just right we first baked the bread, then cakes, and last the casseroles in the waning heat."

Finnish farm women still bake in large quantities, especially before Christmas, since no work is to be done during the Christmas week.

Finnish Christmas Pulla

"At Christmas Mother made *pulla* with cardamom and raisins. Sometimes she braided it into a wreath filled with jam and topped with almonds," recalls Terttu Gilbert. "Cardamom is our Christmas spice—saffron is for Easter. Mother always added extra cardamom to the *pulla* for Christmas. We children loved it with hot berry juice made from black currants and spices for afternoon tea."

1 cup milk	1 tsp. sugar
½ cup sweet butter	2 eggs
⅔ cup sugar	1 tsp. freshly ground
½ tsp. salt	cardamom
1 pkg. active dry yeast	4½-5 cups flour
¼ cup lukewarm water	⅔ cup raisins (optional)
	Sliced almonds (optional)

Combine milk and butter over medium heat until very warm. Stir in sugar and salt. Cool to lukewarm. Sprinkle yeast over water and sugar. Beat eggs. Add milk/butter and yeast mixtures and cardamom. Gradually add 2 cups sifted flour and beat 5 minutes with electric mixer. Gradually add 2½ cups additional flour. Turn out onto lightly floured board and knead until smooth and elastic, about 8-10 minutes. Dough should not stick to the board. Work in raisins if desired. Place in greased bowl, turning to grease top of dough. Cover with plastic wrap and set in warm place until doubled in bulk. Punch down.

Pulla Braid: To make 1 large braid, divide dough into 3 equal pieces. Roll each piece into an 18-inch-long rope. Braid. Seal ends. Place on greased baking sheet. Cover and let rise until doubled in size. Brush with slightly beaten egg white. Sprinkle with almonds if desired. Bake at 350° for 35-40 minutes or until done. Cool on rack and cover with terry cloth towel to soften.

Pulla Wreath: Divide dough in half. Roll out into 8×16-inch rectangle. Brush with melted butter. Spread with choice of fillings (p. 72). Roll as for jelly roll. Pinch ends. Place seam side down on greased baking sheet. Form into a wreath. Cut through roll at ¾-inch intervals. Pull and twist each slice to lay flat. Repeat with remaining dough or turn 2nd piece into *pulla* braid. Cover with kitchen towel and let rise in warm place until doubled in size. Brush wreaths with slightly beaten egg white. Sprinkle with sugar. Bake at 350° for 25-30 minutes or until done. Cool. Serve warm with butter. *(Please turn page.)*

Raspberry Filling for Pulla: ⅓ cup raspberry jam, ¼ cup finely chopped blanched almonds.

Raisin-Jam Filling for Pulla: ⅓ apricot jam or orange marmalade, ⅓ cup golden raisins, ¼ cup finely chopped blanched almonds.

"*MY FINNISH GRANDMOTHER* said they used to race to church in their sleighs on Christmas morning. The first family to arrive would be assured of a good harvest," says Martha Sonnenblick of Los Gatos, California.... Grandmother had another superstition about the weather. If it was nice on Christmas Day, it would be nice all of January. The weather on the day after Christmas forecast the kind of weather we'd have in February.

"In Finland we often make baskets of spring flowers to give as Christmas gifts," adds Martha, "bright tulips, purple hyacinth, lily of the valley, and narcissus are some of the favorites."

72

SHOOTING IN CHRISTMAS had its origin back when Norwegian men used to fire shots out in the yard on Christmas Eve to scare away the witches. The tradition carried over and became a salute to Christmas. Young men, going from farm to farm, would sneak close to the window and fire shots. Surprisingly, the startled family didn't object. It was considered an honor and in turn the men were invited in for Christmas treats.

Many Scandinavian Christmas customs blend Christian and old pagan traditions—lingering from the time of the ancient sun festival, the time of the winter solstice. During those long, dark, cold nights, it was thought the power of darkness conquered light. Witches were about and evil spirits prowled the countryside. Candles, now a welcome to Christmas visitors, originally protected a family from evil spirits.

Liz Nelson's Norwegian Julekake

"This is my grandmother's recipe which comes via my aunt, Hazel Carlson, Mekinock, North Dakota," says Liz Nelson, Los Gatos, California. "She served it on our last visit. I'd forgotten how delicious it can be when baked by an expert like Aunt Hazel." We eat it with *Geitøst*, a golden Norwegian cheese.

1 cup milk	½-1 tsp. ground cardamom
¼ cup butter	½ tsp. cinnamon
½ cup sugar	3½-4 cups flour
¾ tsp. salt	1 cup golden raisins
1½ pkg. active dry yeast	¼ cup candied red cherries
¼ cup lukewarm water	¼ cup candied mixed fruit
2 tsp. sugar	½ cup blanched, slivered
1 egg, beaten	almonds (optional)
	Lemon Frosting (optional)

Combine milk, butter, sugar, and salt over medium heat until very warm. Add raisins to plump. Set aside to cool. Dissolve yeast and sugar in lukewarm water. Beat egg. Pour off milk mixture from raisins. Add milk and yeast mixtures and spices to egg. Gradually add 2 cups sifted flour and beat 5 minutes with electric mixer.

Pat raisins dry. Combine with chopped candied fruits. Sprinkle with 2 tbsp. flour. Gradually add 1½ cups flour to batter. Turn out onto floured board and knead until smooth and elastic, about 8-10 minutes. Work in fruit and nuts, distributing evenly. Place dough in greased bowl, turning to grease top of dough. Cover and set in warm place until doubled in bulk (about 1½ hours). Punch down and knead lightly.

Form into round loaf, pucker side down, on greased baking sheet or 9-inch greased cake tin. Brush with butter. Cover lightly and set in warm place until almost doubled in size. Bake at 350° for about 1 hour or until bread sounds hollow when tapped. Cool on rack. While hot, brush again with butter and cover with towel to keep top soft. Frost with lemon icing, if desired. Serve with Norwegian *Geitøst*.

Lemon Frosting: Mix 1 cup sifted powdered sugar and 1½ tbsp. lemon juice. The top may be decorated with red and green candied cherries.

Norwegian Lefse

After twenty years of perfecting this old family recipe, here are Liz Nelson's recommendations for her finest *lefse*. Earlier, this thin flat bread, baked on top of the stove, was a simple household staple. Now it is a Christmas delicacy. *Lefse* may be served with butter, sprinkled with sugar, or topped with cheese or preserves. They are best made the day before Christmas.

1½ cups instant mashed
   potatoes
1 cup milk

¼ cup butter
2½ cups flour
½ tsp. salt

Prepare mashed potatoes (Liz Nelson uses Betty Crocker Potato Buds) according to directions. (Some *lefse* bakers use fresh baking potatoes peeled, cooked, and riced.) Cool. Scald milk with butter (no margarine). Cool. Combine cooled potatoes, milk, and butter. This will become like a pancake batter. Add sifted flour, a little at a time. Mix well.

With a spoon, dip a piece of dough the size of an egg. On well-floured pastry cloth or board, roll out very thin, into a 10-inch round about one-sixteenth-inch thick. Turn *lefse* frequently to prevent sticking. Roll *lefse* on floured towel and quickly unroll.

Wrap *lefse* around rolling pin and transfer to griddle. Bake *lefse*, one at a time, on ungreased, very hot griddle or skillet (475°) about 2 minutes. When small brown spots appear on underside of *lefse*, turn over, using a long metal spatula. Brown on both sides. Remove from griddle.

If serving immediately, stack and wrap in foil in warm oven. To cool, place between two damp terry cloth towels. Cool to room temperature. *Lefse* should be soft and velvety, not soggy. Wrap in plastic wrap. Place in plastic bag and store in refrigerator. Makes about 12 *lefse*.

Serve warm or at room temperature. Spread with softened butter and sprinkle with brown or white sugar, or top with cheeses or preserves. You may also spread them with sour cream and sugar or with jam.

o   o   o

In Norway all Christmas preparations must be finished before St. Thomas Day, December 21. Wood must be chopped to last for at least the first three days of the celebration. Cleaning and scrubbing are finished, baking and butchering done. At this time the "peace of Christmas" settles over the land.

Sweden's Lucia Queen

In Sweden Christmas begins on December 13 with the Festival of Lights, or the celebration of St. Lucia Day. Although mainly a home festival, Lucia is honored in schools, offices, and factories of towns and villages throughout the country.

In every family the eldest daughter becomes the Lucia bride, wearing the traditional white robe with red sash, the crown of leaves and candles in her hair. Early in the morning, while it is still dark, she goes from room to room with a tray of saffron buns *(Lussekatter)* and steaming coffee, serving each member of the household in bed.

Italian missionaries, coming to Scandinavia, brought the story of Lucia, the young girl who was blinded and died a Christian martyr. Her day now stands for hospitality and light since the celebration comes near the winter solstice, when nights are long and the sun seldom shines on that day. The coming of the Queen of Light promises that light will return.

Old people of Scandinavia once claimed they could see the Lucia bride between three and four in the morning of December 13, gliding across the icy lakes and snow-covered hills in her white robes, her crown of candles lighting the darkness while she carried food and drink for the parish poor.

The Santa Lucia Song

At Swedish Lucia gatherings, young people, clad in white, entertain with old Advent hymns and Lucia songs. They walk in procession, the Lucia Queen leading the way.

Night goes with silent steps
Round house and cottage.
O'er earth that sun forgot
Dark shadows linger.
Then on our threshold stands
White clad, in candlelight,
Santa Lucia, Santa Lucia.

(English words by Holder Lundbergh)

79

Swedish Lucia Buns

"When I was a child in Sweden we ate saffron bread all through the Christmas season," chuckles Margit Pettersson Carlson, Santa Clara, California. "Saffron is absolutely essential for Lucia Buns—there are no Lucia Buns without saffron!" she declares.

Treat your family and friends to Margit's delicacy on December 13. Better still, join the Swedes with your own Lucia Queen serving the family breakfast in bed.

1 tsp. saffron threads
¼ cup boiling water
1¾ cups milk
⅓ cup butter
1 cup sugar
1 tsp. salt
2 pkg. active dry yeast
½ cup lukewarm water

2 tsp. sugar
1 egg
7-7½ cups flour
½ cup blanched slivered
    almonds
⅔ cup golden raisins
½ cup candied orange
    and lemon peel, diced

Soak saffron in boiling water and set aside. (Margit Carlson dries saffron threads in the oven at 200° until crumbly; then mashes them with a sugar cube in a mortar and pestle. She uses additional saffron.)

In a saucepan combine milk and butter over medium heat until very warm. Stir in sugar and salt. Cool to lukewarm. Sprinkle yeast over water and sugar to dissolve. In mixer bowl, beat egg. Add milk/butter and yeast mixtures, saffron, and saffron water. Gradually add 3½-4 cups sifted flour. Beat 5 minutes with electric mixer. Gradually add all but ½ cup flour. Turn dough out onto lightly floured board and knead until smooth and elastic, 8-10 minutes. Gently work in almonds, fruit peel, and raisins, distributing evenly. Place in greased bowl, turning to grease top of dough. Cover with plastic wrap and let rise in warm place until doubled in bulk. Punch dough down.

Lucia Buns: Divide ⅔ of dough into 18 equal pieces, 2½ oz. in weight, or about the size of a lemon. (Set aside remaining ⅓ of dough to make Lucia wreath, if desired.) Roll each piece of dough into a strip, 10 inches long. Form into an S-shape, coiling ends inward (see sketch, p. 82). Place on greased baking sheets. Cover with kitchen towel and let rise in warm place until doubled in size. Brush with 1 egg beaten with 1 tsp. water. Press a dark raisin deep into the center of each coil. Bake at 350° for about 15 minutes. Cool on wire racks, covering buns with terry cloth towel to retain softness. Makes 18 buns. (*Please turn page.*)

Lucia Wreath: With remaining ⅓ of dough, cut dough into equal pieces and roll into ropes. Form wreath according to patterns suggested below. Place wreath on greased baking sheet. Cover and let rise in warm place until doubled in size. Brush with 1 egg beaten with 1 tsp. water. Bake at 350° for 25-30 minutes. Cool on rack.

Lucia Buns are sometimes nicknamed Lucia Cats *(Lussekatter)* or devil's cats—a reminder that evil spirits were thought to be around at the time of the winter solstice when St. Lucia Day was originally celebrated. It is said the devil often took the form of a cat, but his powers could be dispelled by an open display of the same figure—an X with curled tails.

Savor That Saffron

Saffron, the world's most expensive spice, is produced from the stigmas of the purple autumn crocus. Each blossom yields only three stigmas, which must be harvested and packed by hand. 4,000 flowers may yield but one ounce of commercial saffron. Because of its high price, U.S. markets no longer stock it on spice shelves. Customers must ask for it.

"Saffron is now so expensive, many of the Lucia Buns in coffee shops and restaurants are no longer as richly flavored with this spice as before," laments Margaretta Larson, Stockholm. Fortunately, a tiny amount goes a long way.

Swedish Jäst Krans
(Yeast Wreath)

Chewy raisins and nuts fill a wreath of tender, buttery yeast bread. This tasty coffee cake comes from the Swedish kitchen of the late Ruth Peterson of Lindsborg, Kansas.

1 pkg. active dry yeast	4 cups flour
2 tbsp. sugar	1 tsp. salt
1 cup lukewarm milk	1 cup butter or
3 egg yolks	margarine
	Raisin/Nut Filling

Dissolve yeast and sugar in ½ cup lukewarm milk. Set aside. Beat egg yolks until light and lemon-colored. Add remaining ½ cup milk and beat well.

Cut butter into sifted flour and salt and mix as for pie crust. Add yeast, egg, and milk mixtures to flour. Mix thoroughly. Cover and refrigerate overnight. Punch down the next morning. Divide dough in half. On lightly floured board roll one half to 12×18-inch rectangle. Spread with filling. Roll as for jelly roll. Close ends and turn seam side down on greased baking sheet. Shape roll into half moon. Repeat with remaining dough and filling. Cover and set in warm place until doubled in size. Bake at 350° for about 25 minutes or until golden brown. Cool.

Frost with 1 cup powdered sugar and 1½ tbsp. milk.

Raisin/Nut Filling: Beat 3 egg whites until frothy. Gradually add ½ cup sugar and 1 tsp. cinnamon. Beat until stiff. Spread half the egg white on each rectangle. Sprinkle *each* rectangle with ¾ cup raisins and ½ cup chopped walnuts or pecans.

o o o

It used to take a lot of bread for the week of Christmas in Sweden. A housewife might bake from sixty to seventy loaves weighing several pounds apiece for a family of six. In most homes they also baked a round loaf called "showbread," made simply of flour and water, but which was beautifully glazed and decorated with dough figures. Not to be eaten, this showbread was treasured and admired until finally crumbled and strewn across the land to ensure a good harvest. (From a record of a Swedish Christmas 100 years ago.)

EUROPEAN CHILDREN await the eve of St. Nicholas Day as eagerly as American children anticipate a visit from Santa Claus. On the night of December 6 they polish their shoes with extra care to be set before the fireplace where the good saint may fill them with treats and goodies.

Dressed in a dark homespun robe, St. Nicholas and his helper *Krampus* (he's *Swarte Piet* in Holland) go from house to house. St. Nicholas reads from his little black book of the children's good and bad deeds. Obedient youngsters are rewarded with presents—the others may need a birch switch as reminder. Rumor has it that *Krampus* even stuffs naughty children into his bag and heads for the Black Forest.

Shop windows abound with St. Nicholas treats—delicate chocolates, marzipan pigs, St. Nicholas cookies, and sweets galore to fill little sacks. A German friend, Doris Walter, says her grown children *and,* yes, her husband, still put out their shoes for you-know-who to fill.

Just before St. Nicholas Day in Switzerland, bakeries display rows and rows of little bread men called *Grättimannen* (Basel area) or *Grittibänzen* (Bern area). These funny little fellows who beckon with bright raisin eyes and jaunty caps are eaten for breakfast or supper. The recipe on page 88 comes from the dietitian/cook Erika Nussbaumer, who bakes *Grättimannen* for 50 elderly people in a Basel day care center.

Swiss Grättimannen for St. Nicholas Day

These little bread men are sold in bakeries in the German speaking areas of Switzerland for their traditional St. Nicholas Day treat. Large, elaborate *Grättimannen* are often given to children as gifts.

"*Grätti* probably means stickman in Basel dialect," suggests Erika Nussbaumer (who shares the recipe). They are thought to resemble *Schmutzli*, St. Nicholas' helper.

¾ cup milk
⅓ cup butter
⅓ cup sugar
1 tsp. salt
1 pkg. active dry yeast

¼ cup lukewarm water
1 tsp. sugar
1 egg
4-4½ cups flour
Raisins
Egg Glaze

In a saucepan combine milk and butter over medium heat until very warm. Stir in sugar and salt. Cool to lukewarm. Sprinkle yeast over water and sugar. Beat egg in mixer bowl. Add milk/butter and yeast mixtures. Gradually add 2 cups sifted flour and beat 5 minutes with electric mixer. Gradually add 2 cups flour. Turn out onto lightly floured board and knead until smooth and elastic, about 8-10 minutes. Dough should not stick to the board. Place in greased bowl, turning to grease top of dough. Cover with plastic wrap and set in warm place until doubled in bulk. Punch dough down.

Small Grättimannen: Divide dough into 6 equal parts.

1) Roll each piece into a smooth 8-inch oblong body.

2) With the side of your hand, "cut" a head for each *Grätti-annen*, leaving it slightly attached to the body. Place *Grätti-mannen* well apart on large greased baking sheet. Flatten bodies slightly.

3) With a sharp knife or shears, cut arms and legs. Spread legs well apart.

4) Spread arms into different jaunty waving positions.

5) With shears, snip a nose/mouth at the bottom of each face. Cover with kitchen towel and let stand in warm place to rise, about 15 minutes. *(See next page.)*

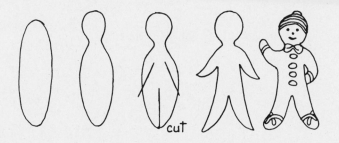

6) Brush each man with 1 egg slightly beaten with 1 tsp. water. Press raisins deep for eyes and buttons. Let rise until doubled in size. Bake at 350° for 15-17 minutes. Watch color closely. Cool on racks. Cover with terry cloth towel to retain soft crust while cooling.

Large Grättimann: Follow mixing instructions. Cut a piece of dough about 1 pound in weight or a little less than ⅔ of the dough. Roll into an oblong body shape about 18-20 inches long. With side of hand, "cut" head and flatten. Place on greased baking sheet. Flatten body of man. Cut legs and arms and spread apart. Continue flattening body and legs.

Form shoes. With small pieces of dough, fashion a stocking cap. Add a little extra flour to remaining dough. Roll out very thin strips of dough (adding a little extra flour) and trim the clothing of the *Grättimann* similar to the decorated clothing in illustration on page 91. With kitchen shears, snip decorative effects into pants and sleeves. Cover with kitchen towel and set in warm place. Let rise until doubled in size. Brush with 1 egg beaten with 1 tsp. water. Sprinkle with *Hagelzucker* or pearl sugar. Bake at 350° for 30 minutes or until golden brown. Cover with foil if necessary to prevent burning. Cool on rack. Cover with terry cloth towel while cooling to preserve softness.

Serve warm, with sweet butter, Gruyere cheese, hot chocolate, tangerines, and peanuts in shell for traditional treat.

A Traditional Swiss
St. Nicholas Day Treat

Grättimännli

Gruyere Cheese

Sweet Butter Curls

Marmalades

Orange & Quince

Black Cherry

Hot Chocolate

Mandarin Oranges

Tangerines

Peanuts in Shells

92

Swiss Birnenweggen
(Pear Ring)

Old Swiss cookery features many recipes filled with dried pears, once a staple in rural households. Pears, prunes, raisins, and nuts hide within this moist, ring-shaped loaf.

Dough
¾ cup milk
¼ cup butter
¼ cup sugar
½ tsp. salt
1 pkg. active dry yeast
¼ cup lukewarm water
1 tsp. sugar
3 egg yolks
1 tsp. grated lemon peel
1 tsp. vanilla
3-3½ cups flour

Filling
2 cups dried pears
2 tbsp. lemon juice
½ cup brown sugar
½ cup prunes, chopped
½ cup golden raisins
1 tsp. grated lemon peel
½ cup walnuts, hazelnuts,
   or almonds, chopped
1 tsp. cinnamon
½ tsp. mace
¼ tsp. nutmeg

In a saucepan combine milk, butter, sugar, and salt until very warm. Cool to lukewarm. Sprinkle yeast and sugar over water. Beat egg yolks until light; add milk/butter and yeast mixtures, lemon peel, vanilla, and mix. Gradually add 2 cups sifted flour and beat 5 minutes with electric mixer. Gradually add remaining flour and turn out onto lightly floured board and knead until smooth and elastic, about 8-10 minutes. Place in greased bowl, turning to grease top of dough. Cover with plastic wrap and set in warm place until doubled in bulk, about 1 hour. Punch dough down.

Knead lightly on floured board. Roll into 20-inch square. Spread with pear filling to within 1 inch of edge. Sprinkle with raisins, prunes, and chopped nuts. Roll up tightly as for jelly roll. Place on greased baking sheet, seam side down. Form into a ring, pinching ends together. With a sharp knife, make crosswise slits about 2 inches apart on top of ring, slashing just to filling or prick steam holes with fork. Cover with kitchen towel and let rise in warm place until doubled in size. Brush with 1 egg beaten with 1 tsp. water. Bake at 350° for about 30-35 minutes or until browned. Cool on sheet 10 minutes. Cool on wire rack. Drizzle with Lemon Frosting, page 75.

Pear Filling: Plump chopped prunes and raisins in hot water. Drain and pat dry. Combine coarsely chopped pears in saucepan with 1 cup water and lemon juice. Simmer, uncovered, until pears are tender and liquid is absorbed. Remove from heat and add brown sugar, cinnamon, mace, and nutmeg (optional: 2 tbsp. *Kirschwasser*). Cool. Spread according to directions and sprinkle with raisins, prunes, and nuts.

"Bread is the head of everything."
—Old Ukrainian folk saying

Among Ukrainian people there is a reverence and honor for bread. More than food, it also becomes part of their religious tradition, used in celebration of life's meaningful occasions.

Ukrainians welcome guests into their homes with an offering of bread and salt. At Christmas, the spectacular three-tiered *Kolach* (symbolizing the Trinity and eternity) centers the family supper table. This same loaf becomes part of a parental blessing when young people marry. *Kolach* is also used in the memorial service for the dead. At Easter, their tall, handsome *Paska* is blessed in church before being eaten at home.

Other occasions, too, merit festive bread. A special loaf at the birth of a new baby. In spring when the birds return, forty birds, fashioned of bread dough, are baked in many households. A farm wife, shaping her bread, cuts the sign of the cross on each loaf. No one gives away the first loaf baked in the oven. Crusts and crumbs are never thrown away.

Indeed, bread accompanies the Ukrainian from birth to death. A gift from God, bread is treated with great respect.

When we sat down to the Christmas Eve meal, my father had prepared a piece of black bread with honey, cut in slices. Starting with my mother and then the oldest child, he went around giving each of us a piece of bread and Christmas greetings, recalls children's author, Marie Halun Bloch, Denver, Colorado.

Ukrainian Kolach

Kolach is a braided ring-shaped bread, used as the traditional table decoration at Christmas. Three braided loaves, topped by a candle, commemorate the Trinity. The ring shape symbolizes eternity. *Kolo* in Ukrainian means circle.

1 pkg. active dry yeast	2 tbsp. sugar
¼ cup lukewarm water	2 tbsp. vegetable oil
1 tsp. sugar	½ cup lukewarm water
3 eggs	4 cups flour
1 tsp. salt	

(For a three-tiered *Kolach*, triple this recipe and repeat directions three times.) Dissolve yeast in warm water with sugar. Beat eggs. Add salt, sugar, oil, lukewarm water; stir in yeast mixture. Add half the sifted flour, 1 cup at a time, and beat 5 minutes with electric mixer. Gradually add remaining flour. Turn onto floured board and knead until smooth and elastic, about 8-10 minutes. Place in greased bowl, turning to grease top of dough. Cover with plastic wrap and set in warm place until doubled in bulk. Punch down. Turn onto lightly floured board.

Directions for Braiding 1 Kolach: (See illustration, p. 100.)

1) Divide dough into 6 equal pieces. Roll each piece into a 26-inch strip.

2) Entwine two strips (rope-like fashion), starting at the center. Repeat with remaining strips, making a total of 3 twisted strips.

3) Entwine 2 twisted strips, starting at the center.

4) Join neatly in a circle. Gently brush ends with water to adhere. Overlap slightly. Set in greased low 10-inch round pan. Leave 1-inch space around outer edge.

5) Wrap remaining twisted strip around outer edge of *Kolach* in the 1-inch space around edge of pan. Place a 14-oz. greased can in the center to keep center open. (Can may pop out if *Kolach* pan is too small.)

6) Place in warm spot until almost doubled in size. Brush with 1 beaten egg and 1 tsp. water. Bake at 375° for 10 minutes; reduce heat to 350° for 40 minutes or until *Kolach* is golden in color. Cool.

Repeat 2 more times for three-tiered *Kolach*. Stack 3 loaves and place candle in center.

The *Kolach* is mentioned in some of the oldest Ukrainian Christmas carols. Round or oblong, these braided ropes of dough are a special delicacy from which came the saying, "You cannot entice him, even with a *Kolach*."

"*ON CHRISTMAS EVE* Dad went out to the barn and brought in a bundle of the nicest hay," remembers Sonja Los Shore who grew up in a large Ukrainian community near Winnipeg, Manitoba, Canada. "We children loved to scatter the hay—a reminder of the stable in Bethlehem—around the living room floor. I still remember its fresh, clean, cold smell.

"Mother did a lot of preparation for this day, baking at least a dozen pies, fruit cakes, poppy seed rolls, and a big braided *Kolach* with a Christmas tree in the center. She stored her baking outside—it froze immediately, it was so cold.

"Christmas Eve the whole family went to church. Dad hitched horses to the cutter. He had built a kind of van top for the sleigh with benches and a little stove inside to keep us warm. We drove in the dark, using the light of the moon.

"The day after Christmas—Boxing Day in Canada—carolers came to our house—two groups—one of young, the other of older men. The young fellows always serenaded the oldest teenage daughter (my sister), taking five steps forward and five back. We younger ones thought that very special. Mother had the table set and waiting with a full meal of cabbage rolls, *borscht, pyrizhky,* and Christmas cakes. Wherever they sang, they were offered a meal. A lot of food, yes! But then, they sometimes walked five miles in the snow between farm homes, so they had good appetites."

Have a Merry International Christmas!

First Sunday of Advent
. . . Gather pine boughs to make a wreath with four candles.
. . . Light a candle each Sunday.
. . . Make a family sharing time with carols, Advent readings, poems, and festive treats.

St. Nicholas Day, December 5
. . . Learn about this saintly bishop.
. . . Read "Festival of St. Nicholas" from *Hans Brinker and the Silver Skates.*
. . . Children put shoes by the fireplace and find sweets and trinkets the next morning.
. . . Write limericks and humorous jingles for small-gift exchange.
. . . Serve a Swiss St. Nicholas treat, page 92.

St. Lucia Day, December 13
. . . Celebrate with Swedes. The eldest daughter becomes the Lucia Queen in white gown and leafy crown.
. . . Serve Lucia Buns for breakfast, see page 80.
. . . St. Lucia Day is the Festival of Light. Fill the room with candles.

Christmas Eve and Christmas Day

. . . Take a walk around the Christmas tree, holding hands and singing as they do in Denmark.

. . . Bake an almond in a Christmas rice pudding. The lucky finder gets a marzipan prize—or will get married next year—or will get to do the dishes!!

. . . Scandinavians put out a birds' Christmas tree, a pole with sheaves of wheat tied to the top. Add pieces of bread, suet, and cranberries for extra treats.

. . . Polish families begin their Christmas Eve meal *(Wigilia)* when the first star appears in the evening sky.

. . . Put a little straw under the tablecloth, as Ukrainians do—a reminder of the manger in Bethlehem.

. . . Set an extra plate at the table for an unexpected guest. Polish families believe a guest in the home is God in the home.

. . . Make a German *Bunte Teller*. On this eve each child sets out a plate to be filled with nuts, candies, cookies, fruit. A tiny gift is beside the plate.

. . . Have children write letters to their parents to be read at the Christmas dinner, as Italian children do.

. . . English children love *crackers*. But not the kind you eat! Small favors are hidden inside cylindrical containers. When pulled open, pop! *Crackers* are part of the English Christmas dinner festivity.

New Year's Eve

. . . In Scotland the first person to come into your home in the new year is a *first foot* who brings a piece of coal, bread, a little money, and good fortune. He is honored with food and drink.

Index